TRANSPARENCIES

TRANSPARENCIES

STEPHEN EDGAR

Black Pepper
Melbourne, Australia

First published by *Black Pepper*
403 St Georges Road, North Fitzroy, Victoria 3068
blackpepperpublishing.com

National Library of Australia
Cataloguing-in-Publication data:

Creator: Edgar, Stephen, 1951- author.

Title: Transparencies / Stephen Edgar.

ISBN: 9780648038702 (paperback)

Subjects: Poetry--Collections.
Australian poetry.

Cover painting and internal image: *Rumours of Light 2* by
Judith Martinez
Cover design: Gail Hannah
Author photograph: Vicki Skarratt

Stephen Edgar was born in 1951 in Sydney, where he grew up. In the early seventies he lived in London; on coming back to Australia in 1974 he moved to Hobart until 2005, when he returned to Sydney.

He studied Classics and English at the University of Tasmania.

His fifth collection *Lost in the Foreground* won the 2003 Grace Leven prize and the William Baylebridge Memorial Prize.

He won the inaugural *Australian Book Review* Poetry Prize in 2005 for 'Man on the Moon', which appears in *Other Summers*. In 2006 he won the Philip Hodgins Memorial Medal for excellence in literature and in 2009 received a second William Baylebridge Memorial Prize for *History of the Day*. In 2012 a selection of his earlier works, *The Red Sea*, was published by Baskerville Publishers in the United States, where he has a dedicated following.

Stephen Edgar's collections are: *Queuing for the Mudd Club*, *Ancient Music*, *Corrupted Treasures*, *Where the Trees Were*, *Lost in the Foreground*, *Other Summers*, *History of the Day*, *Eldershaw* (shortlisted for the Queensland Literary Award, 2013, co-winner of the Colin Roderick Award, 2013 and shortlisted for the Prime Minister's Literary Award, 2014) and *Exhibits of The Sun* (shortlisted for the Prime Minister's Literary Award, 2015).

Acknowledgements and Notes

I am grateful to the editors of the following publications, in which some of these poems have previously appeared: *Angle* (UK), *Australian Book Review*, *Australian Poetry Journal*, *Canberra Times*, *Cordite*, *Island*, *The Kenyon Review* (USA), *Meanjin*, *Southerly*, *Weekend Australian Review*, *The Yale Review* (USA), *All These Presences* (eds Jean Kent, David Musgrave and Carolyn Rickett, Puncher & Wattmann, 2016), *Best Australian Poems 2013* (ed. Lisa Gorton, Black Inc.), 2014 and 2015 (ed. Geoff Page) and 2016 (ed. Sarah Holland-Batt), *A Patch of Sun: Café Poets Anthology* (eds Philip Porter, Luke Fischer and Kit Kelen, ASM/Cerberus Press, 2016), *Prayers of a Secular World* (eds Jordie Albiston and Kevin Brophy, Inkerman & Blunt, 2015), *A Sudden Presence: Poetry from the Inaugural ACU Literature Prize* (Australian Catholic University, 2013), *A Way of Happening* (eds Judith Beveridge and Carolyn Rickett, Puncher & Wattmann, 2014).

Two of these poems were prompted by articles which appeared in the *London Review of Books*: 'The Dancer' is based on a passage in an autobiographical essay by John Burnside, entitled 'Who Chose Them?', 10 September 2009; this essay was subsequently published in his book *I Put a Spell on You*, under the title 'Seventh Digression: On the Mountains of the Moon'. This poem won the inaugural ACU Prize for Literature, established by the Australian Catholic University in 2013. The judge Kevin Hart said of it: 'A formally exquisite narrative poem with all the intellectual acuity one has come to expect of his work.'

'The Life and Times' is based on passages in 'What's your dust worth?', by Steven Shapin, a review of *After We Die: the Life and Times of the Human Cadaver*, by Norman Cantor, 14 April 2011.

'Poppies in the Wind' is based on *Bliss*, a film by Fiona Foley, held by the Museum of Contemporary Art, Sydney.

In 'Et in Andromeda Ego', the first stanza refers to Tom Stoppard's play *Arcadia*.

Parts 1 and 3 of 'Impossible Pictures' allude to photographs by the Swedish photographer Erik Johansson. In Part 3 the phrase 'sky installer' was suggested to me by Carol Jenkins's poem 'Continuing presence of sky'.

CONTENTS

I

II

III

To the memory of my mother
Marion Isabel Edgar
1922—2015

I

Jupiter

The harbour's idle undulations slew
And swill their slicks of glaze to make
An unimaginable shape in time
The mind would ache .
To contemplate. Above, small figures climb
The bridge, aspiring to a simpler view.

Down on the upper deck of the toy ferry
Now sliding underneath that span,
Deep in today's political polemic,
A businessman
May miss the news that renders academic
That puppet show, and makes unnecessary

Proposals he is anxious to embrace,
Initiatives already planned,
Between the tropics and the poles, between
The Ice Age and
The Holocaust, juju and mutant gene,
Planck's constant and the curvature of space.

Tethered in mid-Pacific still revolves
The dateline, dealing out the days
Like there was no tomorrow. Each of them
Plays and replays
Self-replicating hours—a theorem
Of endless present it propounds and solves.

And here, out from the shadow of the bridge,
The ferry surges into this
Ceramic swash, whose crazing would defy
Analysis.
The businessman reads on, but you and I,
Illiterates of trade and leverage,

And risk too intricate for even Lloyd's
To cover, simply watch the slurs
Of gloss and shifting craquelure. They say
It's Jupiter's
Vast mass that draws off, and may hurl our way,
A terminating hail of asteroids.

Under the Radar

Flaring and fading like the blips
That flash an instant on a radar screen,
The bellbirds' brilliant little flecks of sound
Illumine and eclipse
The points where silence has been slung between
The branches of the trees. Such flimsy tips
To bear the weight it gathers on the ground.

As when you wade through water, slowed
And heavy, hardly able to progress,
Your senses, working through this thick dimension
Of stillness, share its mode.
Each leaf glint, shadow, bird note, each impress
Of foot on twig that snaps beneath its load,
More slowly but more clearly holds attention.

Once all the world was this. Alone,
And dozing through the spell of midday heat,
You register that chittering outside,
A neighbour's telephone,
The drone of traffic on a further street,
The ticking house—each floated overtone
Dragged by the soundless groundswell that they ride.

And so it was when you were led
To where her barely conscious form lay waiting
And silence held the burden of the room.
And leaning by the bed,
You swayed in that abeyance, concentrating
To hear far off her scarcely warranted
And weightless breathing falter, and resume.

Bird in Hand

A corner of the eye, or mind:
The shadow-sifting trees?
The flutter of a blind?
There was no breeze.

Some flurry in the other room
Was meddling with the glare,
Which flickered with a zoom
And whirring: there,

In two dimensions on the wall,
A twisting shade transferred
The fluster of a small
And frantic bird.

I raised my arms and waved and fanned
It down against the sill,
And bringing hand to hand
Held it there still,

Feeling the urgent feathers push
My cradling palms. Outside,
At once a rufous whoosh
Opened them wide,

And the fantail was gone. But for
Those moments of close care,
I felt that what I bore
Was less than air,

A nothing formed of heat and flutter,
As though my hands might case
The pulsing shape of utter
Empty space.

Day Book

The heavy pleasure of satiety
Has taken hold, that after-dinner drowse
Around the table in the midday heat,
Half-light defended by the holland blinds,
Their flaring edges always threatening
To yield, and conversation running down
From sentences to broken-ended phrases
With ever longer pauses, until words
And ultimately word-shaped hums and yawns
Must do for sense.

                He pushes back his chair
With what remains of will, leaving the others
Just slantingly aware of his departure,
And makes his way, more roused to consciousness
With every step, along the darkened hall
To the front door, and rashly throws it open,
And reels in the white sunblast of the day.
A photic echo in his eyeballs wipes
The scene before him out. He rubs his eyes.
And now, the gumtree-glazed and muzzily
Outlined dimensions of the light return
With all their depth and form.

                  Some sound, let's say
A bird, now prompts his feet across the loose
Veranda boards and down the steps and out
Into the reawakened and remade
Display of afternoon. It seems as though
The landscape set before him—there, bleached paddocks
With cardboard-coloured fencing, crepitant,

Untidy grass, one carving of a tree,
And here, the scrub ascending into forest
Along the gully, where the sun is from—
This landscape is composed of many layers,
One of those children's books with multiple
Transparencies to peel back one by one
And so reveal some ever deeper detail
Unseen in the whole view. At daylight's pace
He walks out from the house into the bush,
Into the book.

        His own transparency,
This page he's walking, is the first to turn.
His steps go slanting upwards from the ground
Like Wagner's gods across the rainbow bridge
Into Valhalla. And as he looks back down,
First on the glistening, wind-shoved crowns of trees,
And then the massed intaglio of the scarps
And shadow-incised valleys, he is bent
Aside and gradually peeled away
Out of this world of his.

The birds and creatures go on as before
As further sheets are turned: the gaudy parrots
In Faber-Castell colours sweeping past
To smear the sky, a kestrel holding up
A tent of air, and frogmouths, as the dusk
Comes on, their cobweb plumage with its talc
Of mothwing dust and smuts of bark and pollen;
Echidnas nosing leaf mould, possums clumped
Like cushions made of fur in forks of trees,
And stirring now as the descended sun
Drains back its citrine wash. Those claws and feet,

The feathers, fur and skin, the script of bones,
The cursive, hardly mortal helices,
Are printed first in soil, and then in stone,
As one transparent page succeeds another,
And in their changing, simplified gradations
They're peeled away. The songs and calls and cries
That rise and slip across the bent horizon
Leave just the air's inaugural vocalise
Experimenting with the early ferns,
And then bare rock, the sliding susurration
Of ocean upon shore. Still turn the sheets,
In which the hours are aeons and the earth
A molten palette fading to a last
Expanse of starlit vacancy as deep
And see-through as the night.

                        He rubs his eyes
Again, and finds the glare pushed back and forth
High in the foliage, and, leaning there,
Feels the veranda give, and hears its creak
As he shifts his bodyweight from foot to foot.

The Light Tree

And sitting out in our small yard,
As in a cinema,
We'd watch the sunset rays project
The colour of the breast of a galah
Onto a cloud band, or inspect
A sky as yet unstarred

For one faint intermittent spark,
Or turn to catch the glow
That cued our neighbour's eucalypt
To play its slim and stand-out cameo,
Until its crown grew specked and tipped
With stars, the heaven dark.

The light that was eight minutes old,
Light from ten billion years,
On trunk and leafage would impart
Excerpts from their perpetual careers,
So that we almost had by heart
The nightly tale they told.

Those unimaginable laws,
And time too long to mean.
That gumtree's gone. But in my mind,
With sunset's film of aeons, I rescreen
The tree of light and press Rewind,
Or, as the night falls, Pause.

Poppies in the Wind

How long you've lingered here
Has lullingly become
Inconsequent, unclear—
A field of opium,

Nothing but poppies, flowers
That loll undisciplined
Through the slow-motion hours,
Before the time-lapse wind,

Poppies that, row on row,
With poppies in between,
Are nodding to and fro
To fill the entire screen,

With patches of the blue,
Cloud-mackled sky and blond
Expanses glimpsing through
Of the parched hills beyond,

And by degrees the loss
Of petals, the swelling pod,
The ceaseless wind they toss
And bend before and nod,

Poppies that to and fro
Sway in the swaying light
Hypnotically, as though
The whole of history might

Unfold before you, while
The minutes on display
From weeks of days compile
What seems a single day,

Unfold and culminate,
Decay and fall apart,
The blank designs of fate,
Ambitions of the heart,

Projected without end
Across this shifting field,
Poppies that nod and bend,
Their petals blown and peeled,

Nothing but poppies, flowers
That loll undisciplined
Through the slow-motion hours,
Before the time-lapse wind.

The Mechanicals

They built in imitation of the sky,
Or so the theory bids:
The Nile an image of the Milky Way,
And those three stars, their pattern should apply
Beside the river; they
Should model that array with pyramids,

In which the Great House might experience
And constitute the bond
Between forever and what dying means.
Those structures really were less monuments
Than ponderous machines
For transmigration to the life beyond.

Machines. Our means and end. We never can
Exhaust them, or requite
An enterprise no triumph will complete.
And didn't La Mettrie assert that man
Is a machine of meat,
Intricate flesh propelled by appetite?

Yes, but a far more subtle instrument,
Fitted to engineer
From mere abstraction terms to nominate
Itself and its procedures, and invent
The pictures of its fate
In the mind's dark and call them to appear.

Painted upon imagination's wall
Glimmers a faint trompe l'oeil
Through which you might step back to the dawn of time,
Where our first forebears cut and scrape and spall,
In naked pantomime,
The tools to fashion worlds with, and destroy.

Forest Doxology

A little after dawn,
The light a transpiration of the trees
Still misting in the upper foliage
To test the scarcely tinted air,
The adult males are drawn
To lead the company of chimpanzees,
Impelled by privilege
Of status, and the tacit strategies
They've no need to prepare.

So with a knuckled tread
They fan out through the undergrowth, the dense
And incoherent forest they construe
Sooner than thought, and hold a thorough
Picture of. Ahead,
The hunted, whom their cunning circumvents,
Feed on without a clue.
Back here, the camera crew, the eloquence
Of David Attenborough.

But the colobus have seen them,
And, screaming, leap the branches—in pursuit,
Judiciously disposed, the chimpanzees,
Who cut one off within their reach
And corner him between them,
And tear him shrieking, and share out the brute
And dripping delicacies.
So much to plan, so much to execute,
Without the power of speech.

Deep in the forest, so
Jane Goodall tells, there is a waterfall
That plunges in a gloomy solitude
Through the green storeys to a pool
Where humans seldom go.
Here in late afternoon a floating shawl
Of sunlight will intrude
Through branchwork on the water's solid wall,
And rarefy to tulle

The tonnage of its spate,
Shot through with spectral glints and hovering
In vapours, lit within, that haunt the space.
Time and again, when their routine,
And nature, to migrate
Throughout a wide domain, happen to bring
Them near to this charmed place,
The chimpanzees draw round it, quickening,
To see what they have seen.

Transfixed then in delight,
In awe, they stand before the fall and gaze—
At what? The iridescence in the spray?
A presence born of that oblique
Outpour of sun, which might
Inspire, elsewhere, some rite or song of praise?
At length they make their way,
Holding a picture memory replays,
Whereof they cannot speak.

There

It's not the highway that will take you there.
Just peel this shadow back, or step behind
The slant of sunlight on the spathiphyllum.

A stemmed vase? or two profiles face to face?
The squinting, thin-lipped crone? or the long-haired beauty?
Just so, you may be staring at the way

And fail to see it, open as it lies,
A Kafka parable day after day,
To call you in. Or it may multiply

And shift: a swaying blind, the linen press,
A plain brick wall. The password? There is none.
There is no cipher, code or logogriph.

It's not the choice of words, but the pause for breath.
It's not the meaning, but the space beneath
The intonation and the syllables.

Listen. Outside the bank, you may discern
A kind of gravity beyond the vault
Troubling the granite. In the underground,

Hardly alert to it behind the rush
Of air pushed forward by the coming train,
Perhaps you'll bristle for a vast approach

That slips by at a tangent to the hour.
Who knows? From inside, looking out, those locked
Expanses may unfold and propagate

Around, or even through, these episodes
And settings that absorb your field of vision.
A dewdrop there, the mere scale of a koi

Rising to sip the surface, may reveal
The wall, the linen press, the swaying blind,
You and your keenly unobservant eyes.

Touch Screen

And like a scene in which the primitive
Enters the house and hardly comprehends
The way the masters live,
So do the first two days of ours unfold.
We look around wide-eyed,
Housesitting an apartment for some friends
In all its electronically applied
And hard-wired luxury, iPad-controlled.

A touch screen will indulge our every need,
Or idle wish—the merest thought of it
And we are remedied.
The lighting, air-conditioning, TV,
Blinds, awnings, radio,
Hi-fi: on/off, up/down, loud/soft—commit
A finger to the screen and it is so,
Our functions disembodied, virtually.

And then, outside those glass and (strange to tell)
Hand-operated heavy sliding doors
We strenuously propel
Apart to make a wall of vacant space,
The city is displayed
In panorama which our gaze explores
With an extravagance that's half-afraid
We'll blink and find it gone without a trace:

The glassy skyline among which St Mary's
Presents a stone entreaty for the past;
There, skewering midair is
The tower of Centrepoint, positioned where

It claims the centre lies;
Pan right, the bridge and, not to be outclassed,
The Opera House, that permanent surprise;
The green approach to Mrs Macquarie's Chair;

Closer, here are the docks of Woolloomooloo,
And, right below our eyes, the naval base,
At which the QM2
Appears one morning, and is gone the next,
As though it had not been,
Like something one might conjure and replace
With just a finger's touch upon the screen—
A trick to leave us neophytes perplexed.

The light performs its spectral repertoire
From dawn all day to evening. In between
The perpendicular
And cut-out towers, insertions of midheaven
Will sometimes put on view
A slowly moving plane, which seems to mean
To glide by, not behind them, but clean through,
A floating revenant of Nine Eleven.

The harbour shifts its dazzle to and fro.
At night the Opera House appears to shine
With sunlight's afterglow.
This hand I raise and stretch, is that to scroll
The image, or adjust
The settings to accord with our design?
Content as novices, we watch and trust
In what's unfolding there beyond control.

The Knowledge

Again, a sudden shaft,
It stabs right through the picture of the day,
Like sun through clouds, a blinding gash, and floods
Those images your eyes have photographed
And fondly filed away,
In one dissolving glare: the fuchsia buds

Unfurling cochineal
And purple to regale the paling fence;
Star jasmine twining by the studio,
Where she's at work refashioning the real
With facts that she invents.
In one dissolving glare. All this you know.

Or it may burst through sleep
To make the midnight even more complete,
Annul the coloured dream you leave behind,
The bedroom's dark dimensions that you sweep
With blank eyes, and delete
The shadow garden sliding on the blind.

You know all this. Her arm
May rest so close to yours a kind of static,
A subtle current, raises the fine hairs
Along them, like an intimate alarm,
Hard-wired and automatic.
You know this, but record it unawares.

You walk the daylight garden,
This picture you inhabit and compose
And half-imagine nothing will abolish.
Why speak of it? No need to blame or pardon
Your silence, that you chose
The images you have taken in full knowledge.

The Sense of an Ending

Had that been it—
That day at Clontarf by the harbourside,
Out with the two of us to stroll and sit
Beneath a giant fig tree's coverage
And watch the yachts and launches not collide
In gliding process through the bascule bridge,
And dazzle-eyed

See solar flakes
Across the undulating chop ignite
And quench their pyrotechnics in the wakes,
While overhead the swelling cumuli
Constructed at an unimagined height
Their fractal follies out of empty sky,
Vapour and light—

Had that day been,
By some benign apportionment, her last,
It might have held preserved in its serene
And patent field of vision all her days,
Back to the faint horizon of the past,
Her life in memory's amber, where it stays
Both clear and fast.

Only one day
Remains to her, a day she must repeat
Each morning that each evening will convey
Through vacant hours of darkness and restore,
When she wakes up, unaltered and complete
In replication of the day before
That she must greet,

With nothing in it
But her inertia in the nurses' care
And waiting through the weight of each dead minute,
Which with the gravity of a black hole
Draws everything the fluorescent glare
Confronts her eyes with into its control,
And holds it there.

The present that
She stares at and her foregone years are all
One and the same, without perspective, flat
And faded as that print by Namatjira,
Owned for so long (and still here on the wall)
It seems a relic from a nameless era
Beyond recall.

All Hail

After that bigger splash,
Or just before,
The pool lies flat, a plane of blue so brash
The owner must have had a mind to pour
Some concentrate, a mineral to dye
A sheen that was all surface, or
Have drawn off a distilment of the sky.

Persuasive certitudes
Of wealth and ease
And endless summer soothe. Sunlight precludes
The shadow of a doubt. The greenery's
Petalled and perfume-drenched luxuriance
Around the garden wall agrees.
Mid-afternoon hangs languid in its trance.

And a sudden shudder hits
And penetrates
The instant depths of this thin film of glitz.
The light goes dull. A grey pall nictitates
And clings across high heaven to curtail
The turquoise glare and turn to slates
The scalene slicks of shimmer. Wind and hail

From nowhere strike. Golf balls
Of ice, at first
With random plosives, while the water sprawls
In pock-marked shivers, strafe the pool and burst.
And hard upon, to prove it can exact,
And take, more force than this dispersed
Assault, the surface quickens to attract

An ever more extreme,
Thick and intense
Downpour of hailstones, till they come to seem
A frozen photograph—but that the rents
And spurting impacts make the water boil
And splutter with the vehemence
Of pellets flung in overheated oil,

Or something dumped in acid,
A change of phase
Brewed in the chlorine. Battered from its flaccid
And sumptuous repose, the garden flays
Its leafage on espalier and stake.
There's nothing of that aqua glaze
But churning scoria, white and opaque.

The scene is blind with spray.
It's hard to tell
Just where the hail is from. You'd almost say
It isn't from the cloudburst that it fell,
But that the pool in ferment here produces
These icy blisters to expel,
And make away with daylight and its uses.

II

Flight Plan

So, up the rise onto the playing field;
Again, as always, there,
The swallows are before me and revealed
In their designs upon the air.

Quartering the acres with their exact
Asymmetries, they bevel
And soar, and swoop and zigzag and refract
Their flight, bare inches from ground level.

One, just a microsecond from collision,
Jinks at my face to swing
Away, and with a startled click of vision
I freeze-frame the sheer sleight of wing.

Not hunting (I am tempted to pretend),
They're practising some rite
Of preservation: should they bring an end
To their defence of constant flight,

This space might simply perish or collapse—
As now, and now, they dart
Towards a fraying border or the gaps
Where clear dimensions drift apart

And absence threatens to evaporate,
And flying they repair
And bear across the day the empty weight
And formless membrane of the air.

The Art of the Fugue

So, summoned by that call across the wide
And complicated city, pressed
And yet reluctant to arrive,
We found among the ranks of the distressed,
The sick, the stricken and the stupefied,
Her shocked, unconscious form in South Ward Five.
And then I turned aside.

Through the uncurtained window half the sky
Was blacked out over Middle Head
By scarps of thunderclouds; below,
The leaden waters were inhabited,
As ever, by the vessels that must ply
Their patterns, intricate as they were slow,
From far away. Then I

Turned back and changed that vision for the ward.
Nurses, as ever, came and went.
Small groups of relatives stood round
Their proper beds and by a mute consent
Were mutually and thoughtfully ignored.
Doctors with explanations to propound
And symptoms to record

Came also in their turn. A registrar
At last arrived and shone a light
Deep into her occluded eyes
To conjure back her person and her sight.
They looked at nothing in particular.
He asked her what she saw, and her replies
Were very faint and far.

'Too bright,' she said. The sky was out again,
Its heights of lapis copied by
The harbour, on whose sidling sheen
Were carried all the vessels that must ply
Their patterns. It never ends, this regimen—
Then does, as suddenly as fugue fourteen,
When Bach laid down his pen.

Migraine

The very image of escaping heat:
That khaki paddock and the Canberra dark's
High vault of freezing glitter,
The bonfire spilling up its flames and sparks
To feed the stars. The cold
Was bitter.
It seemed a moving picture kept on hold,
To throb inside my head, to throb and beat.

And then there was the trip to Epidaurus
To see *Medea* played in modern Greek
In the famous amphitheatre's
Acute, pin-drop acoustic. We couldn't speak
The language, but took in
The metres,
The drama's overacted bulletin,
The high-flown interventions of the chorus.

And all that day, first inklings on the bus,
The faint sick flicker in the temple, soon
To overcrow my mood,
Growing more potent through the afternoon,
At last to utterly
Occlude,
With nightfall and the play, all I could see.
I felt that fierce thud hammer and percuss,

Until my sense of self had been displaced,
And surging through the circuit of my skull
That arcing pulse held sway.
Recovered, I would stand, reamed out and null,
A weightless revenant
Astray
In my own limbs, to whom the light would grant
Its tainted memoirs. How many days laid waste,

When I consider, by that baleful ache.
And yet the body can't remember pain.
It blighted them, no doubt.
I know it, but the knowledge does not stain
Those images. They glide
Without
Distortion, when called up, and clarified—
Reflexions drifting on a windless lake.

La Vita Nuova

A flock of them that day took to the sky,
The paragliders, harnessed loose and slung
Insouciantly to fly
The steppes of air, those empty replicas
Of paddocks, where their shadows warped and swung
Like a windborne attack.
Above them, though, began to magnify
In roiling folds what was
About to take her life, and give it back.

From all that flight of dozens, it plucked her.
A miles-high mass, it snatched her parachute
At the perimeter
And sucked it in, and up the roaring siphon
Of pressure, hail and black light in dispute
To grapple and transform
Her body to a frozen armature,
Which lofted with her life in
Suspension up to the ceiling of the storm.

Almost an hour she hurtled in ascent.
Unconscious soon enough, with eyelids sealed,
She missed the main event:
The luminance, the lightning-ravished caps
Of clouds. The parachute would likewise yield
And, long before the summit,
Froze rigid as it bore her upwards, bent
Around her in collapse,
Then, spat out at the top, began to plummet

Down all the storeys it had climbed before,
But now outside the storm. Who could have guessed
That falling would restore
Her life to her and thaw the chute, which snapped
Immediately open to arrest
The plunge where she was bound?
With ever wider swoop and glide it bore,
Incredulous and rapt,
Her cold but breathing body to the ground.

The Dancer

I soon had that routine:
Wake; eat; chlorpromazine;
Day room; eat; medication; take a turn
Around the grounds; repeat;
Patches of sleep; wake; eat...
And so on. There was nothing else to learn.
I strayed, unpresent and askant,
One among all the mutually irrelevant.

Irrelevant, askance:
Such is the vigilance
Of those who quit the kingdom of the sane.
Work, the great world's affairs
Are nothing to them. Theirs
Is tendance on the crack in a window pane,
A sister's enigmatic smile
Years past, a headline that conceals a secret file,

Marooned on their own islands
Of individual silence.
One day in the refectory as I,
Hazed with an inward stare,
Sat vacant on my chair,
I felt a sudden presence occupy
The next—our shoulders close, but held
Apart, like two magnetic norths, pressed and repelled.

And stirring to advance
A slight and sidelong glance,
I glimpsed her in a floral dressing gown,
Her hair a dusty blond.

She did not look beyond
Her own held space, and maybe had sat down
At random, not because she chose
Especially me to sit beside, from all of those.

And yet she was aware
Someone, some*thing*, was there—
Not from that outer realm of sense and health;
Rather, a witness, or
A co-conspirator
From her imagined, inner commonwealth.
What she did then played out the script
She wrote there and alone could fathom and decrypt,

An act of her sick mind,
And work of art, to find
And fashion some small order in the chaos.
She rose, and checked to see
That I (or one in me
Whom she projected from her conjured dais)
Was looking at her and, assured
My eyes and my attention watched with one accord,

Began to spin tiptoe
In balanced vertigo,
A dervish, arms outstretched, her body pending
In what seemed, as she wheeled,
To be its own force field,
Sweet as the honey from the sun descending
Through the refectory glass, exiled
But sanctioned in that light, inviolable, wild,

Her whirling fingertips'
Centripetal ellipse
Drawing every glimmering shard and shiver
Of the mind-shattered day
To one restored array:
What she was bound in madness to deliver.
Dark paean. I, who months alone,
It felt, inhabited my own exclusion zone,

Watched and bore witness to
The beauty that she drew,
The wounded state of grace she verified—
Last gift from my unwell
Hallucinated cell,
I thought. The dance was done. I turned aside,
And back, and she was gone, and where
She'd been—a vortex crackled in the vacant air.

Outer Limit

The bird show now begins—perhaps the zoo's
Coup de théâtre. The trainer has by heart
His patter, and each bird its fly-in part.
He winks the barn owl to his wrist, he cues
The Andean condor on spread wings to cruise
Head high and, turning instinct to an art,
Fetch up beside him, marshals the street-smart
And madcap antics of the cockatoos.

The high point, though, must be the peregrine,
Sweeping around an effortless ellipse
To track the circle of a hand-swung lure,
An orbit that her flexing power outstrips
And might well break, to set loose the pursuer,
Though at the brink it deigns to rein her in.

Profane Comedy

The Museum of Old and New Art, Hobart

You even have to get there by a ferry.
It seems a pun on Dante, this performance,
Ironic and askew,
In which the circles bury
From sky and light not veritable torments
But artful imitations, a revue

Of dangers the imagination plays
To please itself. Downward the building delves
In negative, a hollow
And immaterial maze
Winding its way round sandstone banks and shelves.
Crowds mill about the entrance, and you follow.

A lift delivers you to the lowest floor,
From which, in steady spiral, you must climb,
A film run in reverse
Of the Inferno (or
A mirrored and inverted Guggenheim).
You rise and watch the showcased works rehearse,

Over and over, for each passing viewer,
Their single intimation or intent,
That instant, the precise
Image that will endure,
The way that Dante's souls must represent
Forever their identity and vice:

The sculpture of a dangling horse, which sheds
Its form in tearful symmetry, while slung
Suspended from a cinch;
Hundreds of hairlike threads,
Beaded with seeds, lit slantwise—and among
The filaments, transfixed in flight, a finch;

A television programmed to replay
Two figures who approach, exchanging looks,
And—something Beckett might
Have written—turn away;
Or that white library, white walls, white books,
The last fear of the mind spelled out in white.

The body offers up its privacies:
A defecating man, filmed from below,
To which your glance inclines
Against its will; a frieze
Of vulvas, crafted graphically to show
How various is the simplest of designs.

A black right-angled passage you explore
Leads to a doorway, a black room revealing
Another door and room,
And through the final door
The central cell with its black-mirror ceiling,
From which, head down, your hanging features loom.

Level by sloping level, the crowds rise
Towards the ground, the entrance and the end,
And file out one by one.
You pause and turn your eyes
And see the lifts of visitors descend,
Then take yourself back out into the sun.

Face to Face

Still locked up out of sight in memory's attic,
That young bland face continues to survey
What passes through my eyes.
Unlike the picture, though, of Dorian Gray,
It never changes. It defies
The storylines the years inscribe on mine.
With innocent and unemphatic
Persistence, it refuses to decline,
And will not go away.

What, twenty-two or three? That's the consensus:
The age at which the self in the mind's eye
Refuses to embrace
The creases, spots and folds that dignify,
We hope, the ageing face we face.
Before me, I must watch the mirror bare
My falling off and its defences,
But, eyes shut, I can see clear through to where
Those lineless features lie.

I thought I saw my father up ahead
(In my mind's eye, I mean) and wanly smiled.
The age at which he died,
Leaving us speechless and unreconciled,
Was my age now. With one last stride
I stepped through where he stood, and on my way—
A way that was prohibited
To him—till who knows when, although I'd stay,
Surely, his child, the child.

He will not go away. And year by year,
As I outlive him, and myself, the holder
Of an expiring lease,
I'll keep on glancing back across my shoulder
And see the lapse of time increase,
And him no younger. And the face I hide
Behind my face will still appear
As twenty-something, blithely satisfied
To not grow up, or older.

The Life and Times

When all is said and done, what is it worth?
What's left of us?
Carbon and oxygen and hydrogen,
A little calcium and phosphorus,
Sulphur and sodium.
Mere elements. About five dollars, then,
Of value to be turned into the earth.
A tidy sum.

No more than meat and gristle, fat and bone—
Now here he lies.
No consciousness, no point of view, no feeling,
No backward longing look or wild surmise
For what may be in store.
No ghost in this cold chrysalis appealing
To be seen through by love and fully known,
And know what for.

So comes the pallor, now the heart is still.
The blood will drain
With gravity towards the lower side
And spread across the skin its purple stain.
And so the rigor grips,
Though soon enough the body's mollified,
Resolving into gas and grume, until
It simply slips

The complex net of sense it lived to serve.
The rule of law,
The burden of possession are resigned.
The scenes of what he felt and did and saw,
Like boxes by Cornell
Arranged and lit and furnished in the mind,
Go out. No more to see of that *chef d'oeuvre*,
No more to tell.

So many years preparing for this end,
Trying to shore
A memory picture up against this day,
For someone to acknowledge and restore,
As though alive, to sense,
An image they can summon and survey,
Remembering and trying to comprehend
Its elements.

Hearts and Minds

What was that horror film with Peter Lorre?
The man who'd lost his hands,
On whom the hands of a dead murderer
Were grafted (gruesome story)
And rapidly proceeded to transfer
To him the killer's murderous commands.

And yet it's said of heart transplants that patients
Inherit from their donors
More than that vital muscle. They present,
It's said, strange alterations
Of predilection, mood and temperament
(Changes of heart) known to those foregone owners.

The heart, to the Egyptians, was the seat
Of mind, intelligence.
But did they really, locked in silent thought,
And feeling the heart beat,
Sense consciousness behind the sternum, caught
In a cage of ribs, watching, as it invents,

All this? Can we be sure it beats behind
The sockets of our eyes,
The hand-propped forehead, one inseparable
Hybrid of brain and mind
Autonomously humming in the skull?
Too dizzying a crux to analyse.

What if, no neural spectre we possess
And call on to reprise
The fictions of the self in which it's pent,
It washes bodiless
Around us like a primal element,
Like weather blowing through the open trees.

Night Music

The night's blank alleys and blind passageways,
The darkness visible of ruptured sleep,
The hours with their stretched-out and wrung distortions,

Like faces in a funfair mirror—all
Pressed close about this shape of grief. These gaps
And oubliettes and vacuum-sealed displacements

In what I'd once call thought, and thrumming with
The scratched insides of silence and what isn't,
These hollow sockets of each gouged emotion

Grinding their iridescent insect noise,
Their bitter nothings in my skull— they all
Lay down with me.
                    One night I took to bed

Debussy's works for piano, all five discs
Placed round the CD player's tray, all five,
No, more than six surrounding hours. I pressed

First Close, then Play, and then turned out the light,
And went to bed, all eyes in that annulment,
And waited for what might become to come—

The music's heavy water, so I hoped,
Finding its level, seeping in slow flood
To fill and flush those shrill obsessive chambers.

And so, disc one, those stately chords, *Pagodes*
Lapped over me. And wave on wave began
The night's long-playing, alternating phases

Of drowse and wakefulness, the periods
Of indeterminate extent when I
Was absent from myself—or finely snagged

On one still fizzing wire of consciousness
Which pulsed behind the notes its faraway
Demented siren song— then might float up

Midway through *Les collines d'Anacapri*,
Disc two, those runs like startled birds, or hear
Only that whir when disc flicked through to disc.

Brouillards, Bruyères, Feux d'artifice, brief lapses
To doze, and brief arousals, then a deep
Immersion in insensibility

Relinquished by the harping mind, at length
To surface in disc four, towards the end:
Pour les accords. Another whir: disc five,

And *Clair de lune* illumining the room
With a sonic shimmer of forgetfulness.
In one of the innominate small hours,

Succeeding *Elégie*, that final click.
Borne on the music, I went silent too,
My sleep a slowly fading pedal chord.

Mother's Day

Late Sunday afternoon at Shelley Beach.
We clutched our paper cups, the three of us,
And sipped, and stared across:
Queenscliff—so far the heavy metal swell
And overlay of sullen gloss,
Which all those ocean miles impel,
Could almost not maintain the impetus
To reach.

Eerie *Blade Runner* sky—the low cloud smeared
In grey against the buildings, backlit by
The sun's off-colour stain,
Soiled orange symptoms of calamity
Impending, or indeed in train,
Or so the fancy came to me.
But who would indulge a prospect so awry
And weird

In the safe light of day? Who would suspect
That something so outlandish could be true,
At least for one of us,
And in her mind that sky's correlative
Was shining its calamitous
Glare on the day through which she'd live
Quite soon: struck down, deprived of all she knew,
Abject,

Not understanding what she understood?
We sipped and watched the effortless endeavour
Of human traffic there,
Persisting in persisting to redeem
The promise we can't help but share,
Sleepwalking through the daylight dream
Of history that was never surer, never
So good.

Spirits of Place

Still clinging to the folds and bends
Along the little creek, hemmed in between
The fence lines, those brief ends
Of forest look pristine,

From back here, a refugium,
Not just of trees, but of the time before.
That is, until I come
More closely to explore.

Then through the undergrowth, itself
A tanglement of weeds, and in the creek,
Which pools from sandstone shelf
To shelf, at last to leak

Its half-choked and discoloured runnel
Over a sheared-off lip and then be lost
In a stormwater tunnel,
Lies, naturally, the tossed

And crumpled litter, bags and cans,
One rusty shopping trolley, a dumped fridge,
And a length of pipe that spans
The gap beneath the bridge.

And overhead the clouds are cuds
Of sodden newsprint and the sky is drowned
In the dun sludge that floods
The hollows in waste ground.

But over there, on that expanse
Of grass, four herons, utterly self-possessed,
Stand still, and then advance,
And come again to rest,

Absorbed behind the light as they
Inspect the stations of the slope and swale,
And all around the day
Is hanging like a veil.

With slow and ghostly pace they wear
The folds of that grey fabric they step through,
The air, or more than air,
Which seems their substance too.

III

Twister

A reeling blank propped up against
The stretched and livid backdrop of the sky,
It rips, black and top-heavy, through the fenced
And farmstead-mottled plain a path,
This turbine two miles high
Of empty energy
And aftermath,
Debris

Sucked spinning through its hollow core
And flung around a giant centrifuge,
Uprooted trunks and branches, a barn door,
A roof the spooling pressures force
To orbit in a huge
And planetary sweep,
The odd doomed horse
Or sheep.

A planetary sweep. And so,
Our planet rides the empty gale of space
Around the solar system, which with slow
Aeonian rotation runs
The light years round, to chase
The vast galactic storm
Billions of suns
Perform.

And whirling at the galaxy's
Crushed hub, they say, a vortex, a black hole
Is hauling light in, stardust, the degrees
Of Kelvin, spacetime and dark matter,
Beyond the last control
The laws of physics sought,
To tear and shatter,
And make nought.

And so the world. And so the mind
Coils in the gyre of its own consciousness,
Touching on matter to drag up and wind
Around itself (or wind around
The infinite recess
It keeps dissolving in
And is not found).
Here spin

The scene, the utterance, the face,
The sequence, dates you strive to reconcile,
Emotions you unfold, feel and replace,
Midnight obsessions you defer
To your enigma file
And hope the day will solve—
They turn, recur,
Revolve.

Cape Cod Quartet

after Cape Cod Evening *by Edward Hopper*

One

And seated on the step, eyes closed, he bends
Towards the dead grass that obscures his feet,
And sullenly extends
His right-hand fingertips, while with complete
Indifference to his presence there,
She stands and leans before the wall
And window, glowering with an inward stare,
Arms folded to repress
A disappointment too deep for deceit.
Blind-eyed in bitterness,
The pair of them see nothing here at all.

The house, clapboard in rural gothic, seems,
Like them, to be oblivious of the site,
Absorbed in years-long dreams
It can't awaken from. The walls are white,
And white the blinds, and the blind glass
That seals the door is white. All round
The house, a shallow sea of faded grass
Laps at the walls in still
Wind-counterfeited waves, sapped by the light
It trapped in chlorophyll.
In those dry shoals what jetsam may be drowned?

The collie, wading through it, pauses, tensed,
Head turned towards some motion, sound or scent,
Something to warn against.
Behind the house, vaguely malevolent
In its dark, dense encroachment, presses
A forest all of conifers,
Like one of those ensorcelled wildernesses
In M R James—those trees
Escaping from the maze where they were pent,
With baleful potencies.
But for the moment nothing. Nothing stirs.

Two

Massing in ranks of shadow from behind
The house, presses a wood of spruce or fir.
What should it bring to mind?
The one where, by his own dark character,
Midway along his lifelong course,
Dante was fatefully decoyed?
Or mind itself—distress that cannot force
Its way to consciousness,
But thickens and makes ever gloomier
The rooms it can't possess?
A forest for analysis by Freud.

She leans against the window and the wall,
Arms folded tightly underneath her breast,
Wrapped grimly in recall
Of grievances that will not be confessed
This evening, in this company.
He's seated on the step, extending
A hand to brush the long grass vacantly,
Without a word to say.
Nothing they own holds any interest
For either. Anyway,
Neither one is looking, or comprehending.

The house, surrounded by the long, dead grass
And equally oblivious, still waits
For time to—what? To pass?
The dog, adrift in dry haulms, hesitates,
Head turned, ears cocked. Perhaps he's heard
A twig snap, or has caught a scent,
Or seen the flicker of a startled bird.
Perhaps someone he knows
Is coming and now opening the gates.
Over the grasses blows
A breeze as doubtful as this incident.

Three

Dead grass in one uninterrupted sweep
Chokes all the waste that was, or might have been,
A garden, parched and deep
Enough to drown the collie's legs. He's seen
Some movement to his right, or heard
A rustling, caught a waft of scent,
And stands alerted. Something has occurred.
At least, he thinks it has.
In that caesura, poised to intervene,
He waits, unmoving as
The scene around him, and as imminent.

Behind the house, hard up against that wall,
The dreary ranks of conifers impose
Their darkness to enthral
The sorry property. One thinks of those
Imagined forests and what could
Be conjured there and come to pass,
And soon enough of history's haunted wood.
One of the firs is much
More forward than the rest, and one branch grows
Across, almost to touch
A window and its unreflecting glass.

He's sitting. She is standing. Man and wife,
Presumably, and looking as though they
Were sentenced here to life.
Of such concerns the house does not betray
A clue, sunk deeply in abeyance,
Years long, as much by day as night,
And seems to be absorbed in its own séance.
Walls, door and blinds confess
The only secret they will give away:
Nothing. Like happiness,
Though very far from that, the house writes white.

Four

Clapboard rural gothic: the old house seems
Forgetful of itself and of its site,
Sunken in timber dreams,
Which creak to measure time that never quite
Awakens into life, or passes—
While lapping at its walls there came
This stationary tide of drying grasses.
Too late, though, to react.
White walls, white blinds, glass in the front door white,
White as a cataract.
No one looks out from here beyond the frame.

And the long grass, the colour of a biscuit,
Died in despair of ever being mown.
It comes up to the brisket
Of a collie waiting for some yet unknown,
Unseen occurrence or approach.
Head turned, ears cocked, he pauses, tensed,
For this drawn moment to resolve and broach
What must be imminent.
A sound, a stirring that the dog alone
Makes out, a waft of scent?
Something to welcome—or to warn against?

Behind the house, dense, ominous and dim,
Presses the forest, all dark conifers,
Like something out of Grimm.
But, ah, the couple, steadfast ministers
Of grievances they can't express,
Are set in place outside the door
And, locked behind a blind-eyed bitterness,
See nothing here at all.
He sits. She stands. No more. Nothing occurs.
They wait for night to fall.
If there is anything they're waiting for.

Grand Designs

Translated from a northern latitude
And looking the wrong way,
How resolutely those dark cubes ignored,
For decades, how the day
Was offering up its structures to be viewed
From their mean-windowed brick and weatherboard,
If only they would notice the display.

And now at last they had, or those they housed.
The tree line on the hill
Flaring to screen the sun; aquamarine
The cliffs churn white and spill;
The light's sheer pane: they've seen and been aroused,
And dream up grand designs from what they've seen
To renovate their lives with it, until

Their structures and the setting interblend,
Becoming one, almost.
Down come the dark walls, up go planes of glass,
As sea and sky and coast
Surround, then enter and then comprehend
The very space through which these dreamers pass,
The plans in which they're confidently engrossed.

They've seen the view and taken it to heart.
It colours all they do.
Back in the city, working, they contrast,
Consider and construe
How much, how soon, what to conclude, or start,
Just to be home at last, although at last
There will of course be nothing but the view.

Lying in bed, she turns to rest her eyes on
The intermingled blues—
A transfer on the window? or out at sea?—
That pleasurably confuse
The sky and her desires and the horizon.
Or on the deck he scans abstractedly
The future and the shining beach for news.

Small World

Off on the farther shore
Of this sun-varnished lake
The wavelets slick their lacquer in, before
They break.

A slight pavilion juts
Above the liquid gloss,
Supported by a pair of timber struts,
Across

A gap, to reach a small
Rock island. Here trees devise
The sort of gnarled contortions that recall
Bonsai's

Bent practice. On slender toes
Down by the water's edge
Two egrets effortlessly hold their pose
In sedge.

They hold their pose. This show,
With all chinoiserie's
Appeal, must be illusory. And so
It is.

All that the scene contains
In far-dimensioned space
Two trumpery and grimy plastic panes
Encase.

Balsa pared down to suit
Confinement, chiselled fine,
Meticulously fretted in minute
Design—

Trees, egrets, waterside,
Pavilion, lake and sky,
Enclosed within a frame four inches wide,
Two high,

One deep— contrives to give
An air of living day
And skylit time to this diminutive
Display.

Caught in the skylight's glow,
This small world seems to float
Adrift from its housing on the shelf, and so
Remote,

Like the blue distant trace
Of the receding globe
That astronauts watch fondly from the space
They probe.

Woman by a Window

She stands before the window, clear
And comprehended by the light.
It's like a painting by Vermeer,
Where figure, room and things cohere
To fix your sight

Upon their constant, singular,
Intrinsic forms. The studied face,
Jug, earring, letter, globe, guitar,
Are fully, only, what they are
In time and place.

But she belies such calm, her eyes
Dart up from carpet to settee,
To window and the failing sky's
Faint mauve, and scarcely recognize
What they can see.

From miles away she listens to
The Schubert *lied*, recalls a friend
Whom half a life ago she knew,
Rehearses for the interview
She must attend.

Can introspection ever find
A still point in that whirl, or hope
To trace one settled self or mind
In all that jaggedly designed
Kaleidoscope?

Is her imagined self indeed
An apparition, or parade
Of wraiths which alter as they read
The summoned past, then pass, recede,
And are unmade?

When she was young the thought occurred:
This sense of being with my name,
What if somehow it were transferred
To someone else—it seems absurd—
Yet stayed the same,

Still me? And then that earlier day
When she could first identify
That all the rest of them were they,
But, wonderfully, she could say
That she was I.

Impossible Pictures

1   *Watercolour*

Wild night: a gale and creaking timber,
All round the house the spill and slosh
Of water, dreams from which you clamber
Drowning, and sink again, awash.

And in the morning light that painting—
A sheltered bay, the yachts and ramp—
Is welling at the frame and slanting.
The wall is wet, the carpet damp.

2:   *Double Vision*

In the far distance, where the windows rise
Towards the ceiling, those net curtains trail
Across the lowering skies
The rain's long bridal veil.

On the savannah through the living room
Sun shafts and continents of shadow pass
And loom, and pass and loom,
As wind explores the grass,

And from the picture rail high on the wall
The sheer and empty fathoms drop away,
And dark specks loft and fall
Of circling birds of prey.

3: *Walking on Air*

Between twin rows of houses, under
A narrow band of cloudy light,
The sky installer works his wonder,
Laying his pavers flat and tight.

He lays down panel after panel
Of pure reflexion. Where they lie
The street becomes a limpid channel
And mirror image of the sky.

Sunday Mirror

Kerbside clean-up week: the suburban streets'
Tree-lined and mown decorum is debased
With heaps of rubbish that each house repeats,
As though the third-world slum,
Perennially stacked with rancid waste,
It hopes not to become.

The sagging cardboard boxes of chipped plates
And pans, old videos, the broken chairs
And bookshelves, limbless dolls and roller skates,
The oddments that one stores
For years and never uses or repairs,
Keyboards and monitors;

And then the moulded blocks of styrofoam
And labelled packaging indicative
Of shining new additions to the home:
Surround sound, plasma screen,
All those essential luxuries to live
A life that's never been

So satisfied. And next to one such pile
A dressing table, perfectly intact,
With swivel mirror poised, stands to beguile
Each stray particular
The play of light and shadow may enact,
Turning into an open-air boudoir

The length of Sunday morning. Depending on
The angle, in that stare appear odd scraps
Of passing cars, heads, birds, and then are gone,
Like ramblings of a mind,
Or random proofs of theorems, perhaps,
That reason has declined.

Or in the tilting glass the sky processes—
A window looking on a distant view,
Projected film, or memory that guesses
Beyond its own extent
Somewhere for which, alas, the likes of you
Were clearly never meant.

Or every now and then the plain matt grey
That marks amnesia, or oblivion,
As though there were a blank spot in the day,
A cyclic vacancy,
As though it kept forgetting to go on,
Forgetting how to be.

Fake or Fortune

The expert on the TV show inspects
A portrait (shades of Rembrandt) someone's found
Among his aunt's effects,
Peers at the brushwork, pigments, craquelure,
The murky depths around
A face you'd say was struggling to obscure
Its passions, and triumphantly detects

A suspect smudging. He applies some smears
Of spirit, lower right, across the grime
Of centuries. It clears,
Revealing, as those dabs evaporate,
Clues to a shift in time,
The faintest vestige of a name and date.
So the piece is more, and less, than it appears.

New details in the background come to light.
Folds in the gown conceal a different hand,
Now painted out, clenched tight
Around a crumpled letter, so that now
One comes to understand
The glowering eyes, the furrow in the brow,
The mouth fixed grimly in an overbite.

I switch the set off, calling it a day,
Undress and wash my face and clean my teeth,
And partly fade away
As the whole mirror surface fogs with steam,
Knowing that underneath,
When I have wiped that veil of mist, I'll seem
Exactly as I was before, portray

A character whose features are the same.
Though sometimes there's a clear space in his eyes
Through which I may reclaim,
Faintly, some older (younger) self behind
The one I authorize,
Mired in the grimy pigments of my mind,
To whom I fraudulently give my name.

Et in Andromeda Ego

So, in *Arcadia*, that final scene,
Two groups of characters, two centuries,
Possess the stage at once
In temporal choreography between
And round each other. Quite oblivious,
Each mutually spectral pair confronts
The other's living flesh and blood, but sees
No trace
Of what plays out in double time for us,
Bristling perhaps for a faint twist in space.

Once in a while you may experience,
Or, well, imagine, some such incident,
Lingering in a room,
Or close location, charged with an intense
And living presence. You feel, arrested there,
If you could find the angle and assume
The line of sight, you'd witness them, their pent
And pending
Energy reel around you, and would stare,
Half wishing to retreat and half intending

To step into that dance and know their fate,
Those thirty ghosts for each of us alive.
Did not George Bernard Shaw
Say suffering does not accumulate,
The pain of one man is the sum of pain?
So pleasure. And there should be such a law.
For those encounters otherwise would drive
The heart
To breaking, too much pity to contain,
And, in the merging, tear the mind apart.

They tell us in about two billion years
Our galaxy and Andromeda will collide.
No latter-day Big Bang
Will blind the sky, or blast our atmosphere's
Protective bell jar. No, they will unite
In star-stretched emptiness and simply hang
Progressively together, as they slide
Around
Each other's maelstrom of conflating light,
For aeons and wherever they are bound.

The Returns

As then, through smoking fields,
The shattered suburbs and the heaps of rubble,
They still come, shocked by their persistency,

Towards a central square,
In twos and threes, breeze-buffeted companies,
From those twelve points of the indifferent wind.

The city is still there
Of course—or rather, another city now,
Which occupies that name as it does the ground,

And people in whose mouths
A speech still recognizably the same
Sounds not quite right, like a fluent foreigner.

This is no obstacle.
They know the streets, disguised beneath the streets,
Erased beneath apartments, which persist

As rivers do below
The constant efforts of the engineers,
Still flowing through a phantom countryside.

To their uncoloured eyes
This city and the city of their lives,
Like two transparencies of cellophane

Laid one upon the other,
Or heat's warped melting curtain, must be hung
Around them in unstable clinging folds.

And like a sleeper roused
Too suddenly from dreaming, or a patient
A little groggy from the anaesthetic,

They'll briefly be unclear
Of where they are, and when, and whether this
Is memory or their imagining.

But the building will be there,
In one of these two cities, or in both,
Or stretched between the two, a gallery

Of no known space or measure.
And on its walls, row after row, are set,
Like fingerprints in time, portraits of sense,

The disembodiments
Of what it meant for them to be, which once
Were hooked and ripped abruptly from their sockets

And thrown away. Each one
Will draw towards his own, as to a mirror,
And recollect and claim himself again.

On the Beach

The swirling figures in the surge
Of surf are lifted by each wave, and fall,
Dive, tumble and emerge
Through that foam-shattered sprawl,

To form an intricate design
In which they're too involved to be aware,
Motifs that shift and shine
Like water. From the air—

The copter on the shark alert—
Those folding liquid three dimensions flatten,
Which distance would convert
Into a stable pattern.

And from this earthbound distance too,
The nursing home that overlooks the sea,
A not much different view
Extends, apparently.

I see it. But my mother, no.
She faces but does not take in the shore.
Whatever is on show
Is not exterior.

Perhaps the scenes that she surveys
Through inner distance, everything that filled
What used to be her days,
Are also flattened, stilled,

A tableau too remote to reach.
Or is she still among the swimmers there,
Buffeted at the beach,
Swirling and unaware?

Body of Evidence

Lying in bed in darkness, cancelled by
The catalogue of colours, yet I feel
The weighted bulk of my inert physique,
Opaque as barium,
That strand of hair across one eye,
The spasm exercising in my heel
A new and possibly unique
Complaint, the hand I realize is numb
Under the cushioned pressure of my cheek.

The fervid circuits of my brain hum on,
Rehearsing once again old arguments,
Corrupted scenes I summon and attend,
And then dismiss, appalled,
Like some self-flattered paragon;
From their deep archive, shaming incidents
That no revision will emend,
Dredged in their slurry, like that car they hauled,
Disgorging, from the swamp at *Psycho*'s end.

I hear her breathing's syncopated rhythm
Beside me, as she stirs and shifts her knees,
And now that shallow respiration lulls
The workings of my brain.
And now my body settles with them.
And listening to the wind among the trees,
My slowing mind floats out and mulls
The captured and stilled light that they contain,
The centuries they count like a long pulse.

The constellations overhead compose
Their fanciful depictions, which I face
In darkness as I drift off to explore
The night behind my eyes.
Between the pointer stars and those
That feign the Southern Cross, out in deep space
A black and empty corridor
Slides down a sky I'll never memorize,
Silent mnemonic of what lies in store.

Scatter Pattern

It burns a hole
Of numbness in the very mind you use
To hold them safe, to know that those you love
Will be erased from time without a trace.
Of course, you muse,
Clutching whatever fancy may console
Foretasted grief, it's true
That all of history's monsters have to face
Annihilation too,
With all the horrors they were guilty of.

Each cell, they say,
Of tissue, every earthly speck was sent,
And ultimately dust of some dead star,
Intergalactic scatterings which earn us
Embodiment.
There in the glove box of your car today
An atom lies, once flung
From out of a supernova's bursting furnace,
Or fastens on your tongue,
Exchanged in one French kiss, from just as far.

Maybe some flecks
Of mind, no less than matter, do survive,
Some psychic smatterings of fear and danger
Flung from the murderous will of Tamerlane,
And still alive
In your most idle musings. And effects,
The merest motes of grace
Of one it numbs your heart to lose, remain,
In you, yes, but their trace
Dispersed to some unborn and distant stranger.

Printed in Australia
AUOC02n0218070417
284547AU00009BA/9/P

9 780648 038702